Parks for the People

The Life of
Frederick Law Olmsted

Julie Dunlap

FULCRUM
GOLDEN, COLORADO

To my husband, Michael—For all our adventures in parks, great and small.

Many thanks to Alan Banks, Michele Clark, Liza Stearns, and other staff of the Frederick Law Olmsted National Historic Site, to Jeanie Knox of the Emerald Necklace Conservancy, and to the Central Park Conservancy for all they do for parks and people.

Text © 1994, 2011 by Julie Dunlap
Photograph courtesy of Brother Yusuf Burgess: vii. Photographs courtesy of the Library of Congress, Prints and Photographs Division: 5 (LC-USZ62-19200), 8 (LC-DIG-pga-01528), 21 (LC-DIG-nclc-04208), 47 (LC-USZ62-66616), 51 (LC-DIG-stereo-1s01358), 54 (LC-DIG-stereo-1s00444), 63 (LC-D4-9286), 77 (LC-USZ62-87037), 80, 84 (LC-USZ62-94559), 94 (LC-USZ62-971). Photographs and maps courtesy of the National Park Service, Frederick Law Olmsted National Historic Site: 12, 31, 34, 38–39, 46, 74–75, 82, 83, 92, 100. Photographs courtesy of the New York Public Library, www.nypl.org: 16 (Eno Collection, Miriam & Ira D. Wallach Division of Art, Prints and Photographs, NYPL, Astor, Lenox and Tilden Foundations), 40 (Picture Collection, NYPL, Astor, Lenox and Tilden Foundations), 43 (Milstein Division of US History, Local History & Genealogy, NYPL, Astor, Lenox and Tilden Foundations). Postcard courtesy of Friends of Birkenhead Park: 23. Photo scan courtesy of University of Maryland library: 25. Photograph courtesy of University Archives and Special Collections, American University Library: 52. Photograph used with permission of the Society of California Pioneers: 56 (Carlton E. Watkins, The Colfax Party; Stereocard). Photographs courtesy of the Library of Congress, Prints and Photographs Division, Detroit Publishing Company Collection: 59 (LC-D4-9286), 64 (LC-D4-39952), 65 (LC-D4-70287), 71 (LC-USZC4-6887), 95 (LC-D4-36851). Photographs used with permission from The Biltmore Company, Asheville, NC: 78, 86. Photograph courtesy of Dorchester County Historical Society: 79. Photograph courtesy of Artco2/Wikimedia Commons: 90.

Library of Congress Cataloging-in-Publication Data
Dunlap, Julie.
  Parks for the people : the life of Frederick Law Olmsted / Julie
Dunlap. -- [New ed.].
    p. cm. -- (Conservation adventurers)
  Includes bibliographical references and index.
  ISBN 978-1-55591-470-7 (pbk.)
  1. Olmsted, Frederick Law, 1822-1903--Juvenile literature. 2.
Landscape architects--United States--Biography--Juvenile literature. 3.
Parks--United States--History--Juvenile literature. I. Olmsted,
Frederick Law, 1822-1903. II. Title. III. Title: Life of Frederick Law
Olmsted.
  SB470.O5D86 2011
  712.092--dc23
  [B]

                          2011019998

Printed in Canada
0 9 8 7 6 5 4 3 2 1

Design by Jack Lenzo

Fulcrum Publishing
4690 Table Mountain Dr., Ste. 100
Golden, CO 80403
800-992-2908 · 303-277-1623
www.fulcrumbooks.com

Contents

Foreword

I grew up in Brooklyn, New York, in the 1950s and 1960s. As the middle child of seven, I had a tough time finding a sense of place in my family or in our neighborhood, the Marcy Projects. One of my brothers, called "Bird," was warlord of a notorious gang, the Marcy Chaplains. For most of my early childhood, I was "Bird's brother" and safe to walk the troubled streets.

My mother made sure I often escaped the crowded housing projects by visiting Prospect Park. By nine years old, I could get there alone by bus or subway. I would wander the park, identifying trees, catching bumblebees in jelly jars, and filling paper cups with tadpoles to raise at home.

In the park was my favorite tree. I'd climb it and get lost in the canopy, unseen by the rest of world. This was my place to daydream, relax, or travel anywhere I'd read about in my *Weekly Reader*. It's the place I can, even now, return to at any moment when I am stressed or need to meditate and rest. I had never heard of the park's famous designer, Frederick Law Olmsted. What was important to me were the cobblestone trails, the ice cream man and his bicycle pushcart, the butterflies, the praying mantises, and the lady who twisted balloons. Just collecting acorns and acorn tops could be a whole-day event for me at Prospect Park.

Today, as an educator in Albany, New York, I am honored to share outdoor adventures with hundreds of urban youth, some who have never been more than five blocks from where they live. Sometimes we escape the city to camp or backpack. But some of our favorite outings are in Albany's Washington Park. Olmsted's ideas live in that park too. When the teens fly-fish in Washington Park Lake, they reconnect with their own abilities and with the natural world.

I often reflect back to my early childhood in Prospect Park, when my world was fresh and new and beautiful, full of wonder and excitement. I know now that there was a part of me that was innately drawn to nature. Yet many of today's children are growing up in busy cities without nearby parks or special places to experience the beautiful and awe-inspiring. They stand to lose a very important part of what it is to be human. I have dedicated my life to a personal mission: using the power of nature to transform urban youth.

Frederick Law Olmsted began this work more than 150 years ago. He designed Prospect Park–and parks around the United States and Canada–for city kids like me, who would need outdoor places to explore and run free. Children will still need to find a sense of place 150 years from now. Learning about Olmsted and the history of parks will help us make sure there are always parks for all the people.

–Brother Yusuf Burgess,
Board Member, Children
& Nature Network;
Family Intervention
Specialist, Green Tech
High Charter School
Albany, New York

Introduction

Parks come in all shapes and sizes. Some have just enough room for a few benches or a basketball court. Others, such as New York's Central Park, cover acres with lakes, woods, and meadows. Some city parks, such as those in Boston's Emerald Necklace, are linked so people can walk for miles under a canopy of green. And in places like Yosemite National Park, visitors can roam for days in near wilderness.

In the early 1800s, no one could imagine such parks. Most Americans lived on farms or in small towns. Farmers had wild animals, forests, and open spaces all around them. Town families often had gardens and barns, and the countryside was just a short walk away. Parks didn't seem necessary.

But America was changing. Cities were growing rapidly, and the new residents often lived in crowded, dirty slums. Rich people in cities could take country vacations, to breathe clean air and rest from the noise and stress. But for the urban poor, there was no escape.

Frederick Law Olmsted thought cities could—and *must*—be changed. People need cities, he agreed, but cities need parks. Fred designed parks of all kinds, transforming the way our cities and country look and feel. Today, in the twenty-first century, many of the parks he created are even more beautiful than when they were built. Fred was a nineteenth-century artist and pioneering conservationist. And as our nation and world grow busier and more complex, Frederick Law Olmsted's work grows more important than ever.

1
Free to Roam

Fred Olmsted sat on the edge of the stagecoach seat, chattering to his father about their trip. How exciting to see the towns and forests of western New York! John Olmsted, Fred's father, smiled at his six-year-old son's restless enthusiasm.

Suddenly, Fred stopped talking. That roar in the distance could only be one thing. Niagara Falls! The moment the stage stopped, Fred scrambled out the door

Travelers from around the world came to admire the wild beauty of Niagara Falls in 1828, the year young Fred first saw it.

and raced down a wooded path to a rocky overlook. There, he stopped still. Before him a broad, green river swirled around boulders and forested islands until it crashed over the edge of the falls. In the mist churned up by the pounding water, a pale rainbow sparkled. Never would Fred forget that magnificent scene.

Born on April 26, 1822, Fred lived four hundred miles from Niagara Falls, in Hartford, Connecticut. Olmsteds had already lived there for seven generations when young Fred was born. The little boy often walked alone down the shady streets of the small, thriving city. Among the fine homes, churches, and shops he passed was a store belonging to his father. John Olmsted sold dry goods—mostly cloth and sewing supplies. Profits from the store allowed John to support a large family comfortably.

Fred and three-year-old John Hull Olmsted were the only children from their father's first marriage. Their mother, Charlotte Hull, had died when Fred was only three, leaving both boys stricken with grief and dependent on each other. Yet after their father's second marriage, they learned to call their stepmother, Mary Ann, Mother. The family expanded until the boys had six half sisters and brothers— Charlotte, Mary, Bertha, Owen, Ada, and Albert.

John and Mary Ann loved all their children,

but Fred's tireless energy sometimes tried their patience. With so many little ones to care for, they often left their eldest to roam on his own. At daybreak, he would shove some crackers into his pockets and head down a city street or a dirt road into the country. His parents always trusted that Fred's good sense and kind neighbors would keep him safe.

On his walks, he picked wildflowers and chased rabbits. No fox track or woodpecker hole escaped his keen blue eyes. His ears heard every hawk's cry. More than once, he got lost. But Fred would rap on a stranger's door to ask for a bed that night, then head cheerfully home in the morning.

When he could not go out exploring, Fred found ways to enjoy nature close to home. He pestered an uncle into lending him garden space to grow flowers. An elderly neighbor liked having the curious boy around and let him study a personal museum of butterflies, rocks, and plants. On rainy days, Fred might dig through his grandfather's attic, then pore over Captain Olmsted's sea charts and imagine an ocean voyage. Or he headed to a Hartford library to read a favorite book, *Forest Scenery*. Fred marveled that the author made the English countryside seem almost as magical as Niagara Falls.

In the 1830s, Fred's hometown of Hartford was a busy port on the Connecticut River surrounded by woods and farm fields.

Fred's parents liked the outdoors almost as much as he did. Never talkative, John Olmsted did not speak about why woods, mountains, and night skies meant so much to him. But he shared his love of wild places with his children as often as he could. Whenever John could get away from the store, he piled the whole family into the carriage. The Olmsteds bounced down rutted roads toward the Connecticut River for a picnic, a swim, or a few hours of berry picking. At a time when few people traveled far from home, the family ventured to the White Mountains, New York's forests, and the coast of Maine.

Yet while John shared his son's love of exploring, he also worried about his unruly eldest child. A dedicated Congregationalist, John believed that Fred had a duty to God to help the world—to study hard and learn a useful profession. John regretted his own poor education and dreamed that someday his son would study at Yale College. Perhaps he would be a scholar, like his uncle Jonathan Law, and a community leader. But the first schools the boy tried could not contain his antics. So Mr. Olmsted sent Fred to live and study with a nearby parson.

The parson was also a farmer, and seven-year-old Fred spent more time doing chores than studying Bible verses. He gladly helped his teacher pick apples and cart them to the cider press that fall. In late winter, he hauled buckets to collect maple sap and tasted hot syrup in the sugaring shack. After washing and shearing sheep in the spring, he joined neighbor boys to smoke woodchucks out of their burrows. When the earth warmed in the summer, Fred kicked off his shoes and explored the fields barefoot.

The farm work delighted Fred, but his father was dissatisfied. *The boy needs discipline*, he thought.

The Hartford school that Fred went to next also disappointed John. Then he sent Fred to a boarding school. Bullies teased the new pupil, the smallest of the sixty boys. The teachers also punished the students cruelly. Fred refused to complain, but a classmate wrote Mr. Olmsted that one teacher had lifted Fred by the ears and pinched them until they bled. Furious, Fred's father came to take him home.

Finally, John chose a small school run by Reverend Joab Brace. Nine-year-old Fred and three other boys studied and slept in Reverend Brace's drafty schoolroom. When winter winds whistled through the cracks, the boys huddled around the tiny woodstove to memorize their lessons. Reverend Brace punished every mistake with a sharp rap on the knuckles. A shivering Fred struggled to learn psalms and Latin grammar rules, but his mind kept drifting. How he longed for the summer woods!

Sometimes, Fred told stories to cheer up the other students—usually about running away from school. But Reverend Brace checked to make sure the boys were studying. He slipped off his shoes before tiptoeing up the wooden stairs to listen at their door. If he heard talking, the reverend would burst into the room, shouting, "Oh! The depravity of human nature!" Grabbing a broomstick, he beat his students on their shoulders. Fred quickly learned to dodge around Brace's legs and run to the barn, where he burrowed deep into the hay.

For four years, Fred saw his family only briefly on holidays and summer vacations. One summer Sunday, Fred's grandfather found him lying beneath an elm tree, watching its branches swaying in the breeze. Captain Olmsted told Fred about planting the sapling himself as a boy. Fred realized that nothing in his grandfather's long life had made him prouder than planting that tree.

Too soon for Fred, it was time to go back to Reverend Brace's. School improved a bit in 1835, when his brother John joined him. Always close, the boys became study partners and best friends.

When fourteen-year-old Fred returned home that summer, he headed straight for the woods. Overjoyed to be free from school, he did not notice when he walked through a path of a sticky plant called poison sumac. An itchy rash soon covered his arms and face. By the next day, Fred's eyes were nearly swollen shut.

Even a week later, his eyes were still swollen and painful. The doctor worried that Fred's sight might be permanently damaged. *You must rest your eyes*, the doctor warned. *No more studying!*

Fred (sitting, right) posed with his brother, John Hull, (standing, right) and friends while taking classes at Yale in 1846.

At first, Fred was thrilled. No more Reverend Brace! Instead, hoping to help Fred heal, his father sent him to be an apprentice with a civil engineer in Massachusetts. Learning to make maps and draw imaginary roads and towns was great fun. Long hours tramping across the fields, measuring the shape of the land, made him feel strong and healthy again.

But now Fred, even more than his father, began to worry about the future. Friends and even his younger brother were studying hard to prepare for college. Like John Olmsted, Fred felt he had a duty to help others. But if he couldn't learn a profession at Yale, Fred wondered, what could he do?

2

Restless Spirit

Fred perched on a high stool, scratching columns of numbers with a quill pen. His father had brought him to New York City in 1840 to work at Benkard and Hutton, a French dry-goods importer. There, John hoped, his son would learn how to run a business. Fred tried to like the job to please his father, but he felt trapped in the dull, stuffy office.

Fred cheered up, though, whenever the boss sent him to check in a new shipment at the East River wharves. A forest of masts lined the docks, and flags of ships from all over the world snapped in the breeze. Once Fred found his ship, each bale of cloth for Benkard and Hutton had to be carefully inspected. But his eyes kept wandering to watch the sailors. As the ship rocked gently on its moorings, Fred's heart filled with longing for the sea.

Traffic noise hurt his ears as he walked back to the store. New York's streets stank from horse manure and rotting trash, and pigs rooted in the slop. Tall buildings blocked out the sun, making the straight, narrow roads feel like crowded tunnels. People from around the world were drawn to the fast-growing

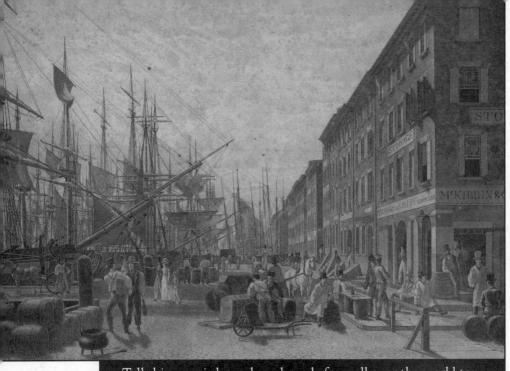

Tall ships carried people and goods from all over the world to New York City's bustling South Street Seaport in the 1840s.

city in hopes of finding jobs. But many ended up living in ghettos, unemployed or laboring long hours for little pay. Fred had enough money to get by, but he felt the tension and unhappiness of his neighbors. Their frustrations sometimes erupted into angry riots. How Fred missed his Hartford hometown, where even poor people could take a country walk to revive.

Life as a city clerk was not for him, Fred decided. Why not go to sea like Grandfather Olmsted? In spring, a merchant ship would sail from New York Harbor to trade with China. Captain Fox of the *Ronaldson* warned the soft-handed office clerk, "We always dislike to take a green hand." But Fred was determined to go.

He crammed a sea chest with flannel shirts, duck pants, an oil suit, and a remedy for seasickness. On April 23, 1843, Apprentice Seaman Olmsted set sail, three days before his twenty-first birthday.

A few days into the voyage, a gale began to toss the ship. Heavy waves broke across the deck, soaking the crew to the skin. Desperately seasick, Fred crawled into a cramped berth below deck. By the time Fred felt well enough to eat, the fresh food was gone. What remained was a grim diet of salt beef, sea biscuit, and sour gruel. Too weak to climb aloft, he was put to work filing rust off tools.

The *Ronaldson* rounded Africa's Cape of Good Hope and sailed through the Java Sea. In Canton, China, Captain Fox traded his cargo of ginseng for tea and raw silk. To speed the return voyage, the captain worked his crew harshly. Though sick with scurvy from the poor diet, Fred took his turn trimming the sails, pumping bilge water, and keeping sharp lookout. Later, Fred told his parents, "We were often kept at work with scarce a minute's rest." Exhausted, on one night watch he fell asleep standing up. When the ship finally docked in New York City, John Olmsted did not recognize his gaunt, pale son.

After a punishing year at sea, Fred hunted for work on dry land. *Perhaps farming is worth a try*, he thought. To get started, he visited the farms of Connecticut friends and neighbors. Next, he listened in on a few classes on scientific farming at Yale, where his brother John was earning a degree.

To get real farming experience, he apprenticed at George Geddes's prizewinning farm in New York State. Fred asked George a crop of questions about how to choose the best plants, how to enrich poor soil, and how to drain soggy fields. Fred planted and fertilized and hoed and harvested until his back ached.

Letters home were filled with mouthwatering lists of food he was growing—green peas, melons, sweet corn, tomatoes, cherries. Raising food made him feel useful, Fred wrote. Plus, he could work outside, surrounded by fresh air and beautiful scenery.

Fred's enthusiasm convinced his generous father to give him money to buy his own land (and a huge farm dog named Neptune). Fred's first farm on the Connecticut shore was too rocky to grow much, but in March 1848, he (and Nep) moved to richer land on Staten Island. From his porch, he could watch ships in New York Bay.

There was little time, though, to admire the view. The fields and buildings had been badly neglected. With a large crew of hired hands, he drained wet fields and planted acres of hay, corn, and oats. The fall harvest was bountiful.

At night he sat by the hearth, reading about the latest scientific farming ideas. His favorite magazine was *Horticulturist*, edited by Andrew Jackson Downing. A famous landscape gardener, Downing advised farmers to plant trees, bushes, and flowers around their homes. Landowners, he wrote, should bring nature's beauty up to their doors. Downing's words inspired Fred. As the fire burned to embers, the young farmer sketched out plans to beautify his land.

Fred set a crew to work moving the barns out of sight and building a gracefully curving, tree-lined driveway. To shade the farmhouse, he planted walnut, elm, and mulberry trees. Soon Fred's acres looked so much better that neighbors asked his advice about their land. Fred gave it eagerly.

John Hull Olmsted, always more focused than his brother Fred, was now a medical student in New York City. The sooty air bothered his lungs, and he escaped on weekends to Fred's farm. A nagging cough kept John from helping with chores, so while Fred plowed and planted, John talked with a charming seventeen-year-old neighbor, Mary Perkins.

When John and Mary became engaged, Fred was happy for them—but not envious. Those intense blue eyes had captured the hearts of a few girls, but he was too in love with farm work to want romance.

Another frequent farm visitor, Fred's father, also celebrated the engagement. One son would soon be a happily married doctor. The other was creating a beautiful, prosperous farm. Their future looked secure.

But despite Fred's love of farming, his restlessness returned. In 1850, John Hull announced plans to tour England with a Yale friend, Charles Loring Brace, before getting married. Fred talked his father into sending him along to watch over John's poor health.

Expecting the English countryside he had read about in *Forest Scenery*, Fred was shocked by his first glimpse of England. In Liverpool, a fast-growing port city, coal smoke hung thick in the air. Filthy water ran in the gutters, and the only animals around were rats. On tenement steps sat women dressed in rags, watching children dodge carriages to play in the streets. The poverty and pollution were even worse than in New York. He wondered, *Does city living have to be so miserable?*

Fred, John, and Charles escaped Liverpool to tramp down shady country lanes, their spirits lifting as they smelled the clover. But it disturbed Fred that the

Poor people in England, New York, and other cities breathed dirty
air in crowded slums, and children played in littered, busy streets.

prettiest places were closed to the public. Many wealthy landowners created wooded gardens, called deer parks, for private hunting. *Why should the rich have these parks,* he asked himself, *while the poor must play in the streets?*

One day, the travelers wandered into Birkenhead, a new town outside Liverpool. The town boasted one of the first parks for the public in England. The park's designer, Joseph Paxton, was a gardener, engineer, and architect. He had needed all his skills to create the rolling park landscape from flat farmland. Hills and valleys had been molded out of dirt dug to build two lakes, and winding gravel paths carried buggies and horseback riders past sweeping lawns and through groves of trees. In the open spaces, city boys played cricket, girls rolled hoops, and toddlers tumbled in the grass. Poor people as well as rich strolled in the sunshine.

If only New York City had a public park like this, Fred thought, *where poor laborers could rest and breathe clean air.* "I have seen nothing in America so fine," Fred declared.

In his diary, Fred wrote about Birkenhead's People's Park and the problems he saw in England. Once home again, he decided to turn his journal into a book. *Walks and Talks of an American Farmer in England,* published in 1852, impressed critics. Andrew

Jackson Downing praised the book as "fresh and honest." Although few copies were sold, Fred had a new direction. A writer, he believed, could do more to solve America's problems than a farmer.

A newspaper editor liked the book. He asked

10,000 people celebrated the 1847 opening of England's Birkenhead Park, and Fred admired "how art had been employed to obtain from nature so much beauty."

Fred if he could write about the biggest problem in 1850s America: slavery. Fred had once said that he would break the law to hide a runaway slave, and his good friend Charles Brace was an outspoken abolitionist. Fred opposed slavery, but didn't know what to do about it. A war to end slavery could destroy the country, he feared. Taking the reporting job would mean a chance to sort out his conflicted feelings by learning about slavery up close.

In December 1852, Fred set off on horseback for a four-month journey through the South. From plantation after plantation, Fred mailed north drawings and stories about crude cabins, meager food, and whippings suffered by slaves. But Fred grew to believe that the owners' worst cruelty was depriving black people of liberty. Even under the kindest masters, he wrote, slaves suffered in "mind and soul."

Articles in the *New-York Daily Times* opened many readers' eyes to the realities of slavery. To convince more people, he took more trips by rail, steamboat, and on foot. In Texas with John Hull, Fred camped in the wilderness and felt a sense of freedom that contrasted sharply with the lives of slaves they met.

Writing let his voice against slavery be heard as far away as England. His second book, *A Journey in the Seaboard Slave States*, won Fred acclaim from many northern reviewers (southern critics called the book unfair). Like his first book, though, it did not sell many copies.

Fred's spirits sank. No matter how hard he worked, he could not support himself as a writer. His neglected farm no longer interested him; he handed it over to the newlyweds, John Hull and Mary. Then he borrowed more money from his father to buy part of a publishing firm. Fred devoted his energies to editing *Putnam's Monthly Magazine*, a leading journal that published Henry Thoreau, Herman Melville, and other American writers. But the company went bankrupt.

Fred sketched black slaves being threatened by a white overseer for his book *Journey in the Seaboard Slave States*.

At thirty-five, Fred feared that even his patient father believed him a failure. Still worse, his family was too far away to comfort him. John Olmsted had taken John Hull, Mary, and their children to Europe in the frantic hope of healing his son's tuberculosis. To Fred, the future had never looked so bleak.

3

Green Island
in the City

In August 1857, Fred retreated to a Connecticut sea-side inn to finish his latest book. Lonely and discouraged, he was glad to meet an old friend, Charles Elliott. Charles was one of eleven commissioners working to set up a brand-new park in New York City.

New York had grown enormously since Fred's days as a dry-goods clerk. Thousands more immigrants, jobless laborers, and former slaves crowded into its slums every year. The only places poor New Yorkers could rest or play outdoors were a few neighborhood squares or cemeteries. Some city leaders had been campaigning for years for a large public park like England's Birkenhead. Andrew Jackson Downing, the landscape gardener Fred so admired, had backed the idea before he died in a steamboat accident. Fred's *Walks and Talks* had added another important call for city parks.

Not everyone wanted a park, though. Some businessmen thought it would cost too much and take up land that should be used for businesses that could make money. But the park idea had become popular with voters. In 1856, the city bought 778 acres for a park in the center of Manhattan Island. (Building developers did not want that rocky, swampy place anyway.)

The Central Park Commission hired an engineer, Egbert Viele, to begin planning and construction. As Charles Elliott told Fred, the engineer needed a superintendent to oversee workers clearing the grounds. Impressed by Fred's farming experience and love of parks, Charles encouraged him to apply for the job.

It would take hard work to get hired. The commissioners, Fred knew, would wonder whether a clerk-turned-sailor-turned-farmer-turned-writer would have the skills to manage rough labor gangs. With a petition in hand, he searched New York City for friends to recommend him. Many people admired Fred's books and were happy to sign. It was probably the signature of Washington Irving—famous author of "The Legend of Sleepy Hollow"—that persuaded the commissioners to hire Fred.

Park engineer Viele still doubted Fred's abilities. On a hot September afternoon, Superintendent Olmsted arrived at their first meeting wearing his finest suit. Viele smirked at this fancy-dressed writer posing as his assistant. Viele put a laborer in heavy

For some men in the labor gangs building Central Park, Fred's fancy clothes disguised his toughness and determination.

boots in charge of Fred. The man trudged into the messiest parts of the park, slogging through steaming bogs once used for pigsties and slaughterhouses. Fred held his tongue but later admitted, "The stench was sickening." Standing knee-deep in black slime, he could hardly imagine a worse place for a park.

Laborers he passed laughed at their mud-spattered new boss. Most of the men had been given their jobs as favors from politicians who wanted their votes. They did their work—tearing down fences, removing trash, and rounding up goats left by former residents—slowly and carelessly. No one worried that the refined young superintendent would make them work harder.

Fred was tougher than he looked and determined to surprise them all. Once an undisciplined boy himself, he saw the laborers needed a firm hand. So he set up strict rules: each man must arrive on time, obey orders, and not stop work without permission. Crew foremen must watch each worker's behavior and report daily to Fred. Anyone who wouldn't follow the rules would be fired.

Soon, on daily inspection walks, Fred (now in heavy boots of his own) found crews grubbing out tree stumps, carting stones, burning brush, or yanking out poison ivy. Each crew foreman nodded respectfully to Mr. Olmsted as he passed.

Fred loved his job. He later wrote, "If a fairy had shaped it for me, it couldn't have fit me better." But his salary was small. He had to borrow money for a horse and do without a warm hat. And every day, he anxiously awaited the mail, hoping for word from his brother. John was now in France, still battling his tuberculosis.

Finally, a letter arrived. "Dear dear Fred," John wrote. "It appears we are not to see one another any more—I have not many days, the Dr says." He reminded Fred of their happy times together, writing, "I never have known a better friendship than ours has been." His last request to Fred was to watch over his wife. "Don't let Mary suffer while you are alive." A few days later, John died quietly with his father and wife at his side.

The blow to Fred was deep. He hid from the grief by working harder. When the park commission announced a contest for the final park design, he was too busy with construction to think of entering. But one day, a young English architect interrupted him. Calvert Vaux had been Andrew Jackson Downing's partner, designing elegant homes for estates landscaped by Downing. Calvert knew how to plan a large project, he told Fred, and how to design bridges, roads, and buildings. But Fred knew the park grounds better than anyone. Would Fred help him design an entry? The tiny but forceful Calvert talked Fred into trying. (The $2,000 prize helped convince him too.)

Calvert Vaux was already a well-known architect when he convinced Fred to help him design Central Park.

At night after work, the men explored the grounds and discussed their ideas. Both tried to think like sculptors. How could they shape this barren place into a beautiful, useful park? Calvert pictured the park as a masterpiece of country scenery. Fred imagined a country refuge–where both poor and rich could escape the city's noise, dirt, and hectic pace.

They began spending evenings bent over Calvert's drafting table, sketching ideas until their fingers throbbed. Fred loved the detailed work! Sometimes, their throats ached, too, from arguing over which ideas to put in and which to leave out. Later, no one was quite sure who had designed which parts.

Slowly, their ideas and sketches turned into a plan. Sights and sounds of the city, they decided, should be blocked by a thick border of trees. Four roads through the park should be sunk below ground level to protect visitors from city traffic. In the north, sweeping green meadows would let city people stroll through peaceful countryside.

Dense woods on a rugged southern hillside would give everyone a wilder place to ramble. The trees would serve as "lungs of the city," cleaning the air for everyone. Nearby would be a cricket field, a space for concerts, and a lake for boating in summer and skating in winter.

The contest deadline approached. Fred and Calvert quickly drew "before" and "after" sketches, showing how the grounds would change (Calvert probably did most of the drawing–he was a more talented art-ist). They worked feverishly on a long report that described their ideas, listed plants to use, and tallied construction costs. Friends who dropped by were even asked to pick up pens and draw grass into the twelve-foot-long park plan. The partners refined their entry up until the contest's final minutes.

On April 1, 1858, they submitted their pro-posal–the Greensward Plan–the last of thirty-three entries received.

Competition was stiff. Some designers suggested turning the space into an enormous amusement park. Another offered plans to build a vast formal garden. Which plan would be best for New York? After four long weeks of debate, Greensward won first prize.

Fred and Calvert split the prize money and shared the joy. The commissioners were so pleased with the plan that they fired engineer Viele, pro-moted Fred to architect-in-chief, and hired Calvert as architectural assistant.

Calvert would always be envious that Fred was promoted above him, and Fred disliked his job title too. He thought of architects as people who design buildings. But he was not a landscape gardener either. Planting trees and flowers was just part of the art and science of making a park.

Fred and Calvert knew they were helping invent a new profession. They decided to call themselves landscape architects, designers of outdoor places for public use and enjoyment.

This was just the work he had been looking for, Fred thought. And John Olmsted, reading letters about his son's happiness and accomplishments, breathed a sigh of relief.

Park construction began in earnest. Engineers laid miles of pipe to drain swamp water into the newly dug lake. Explosions echoed as crews blasted out the sunken roads. Three thousand laborers–gardeners, road builders, blacksmiths, carpenters, wagon drivers, stone breakers–worked under Fred's authority to shape the park.

In the midst of construction, Fred thought about future park visitors. Since few Americans had ever been to a park, Fred expected people might not know how to act. So he posted signs:

Central Park Visitors are Warned
Not to walk upon the grass; (except of the Commons);
Not to pick any flowers, leaves, twigs, fruits or nuts;
Not to deface, scratch, or mark the seats or other constructions;
Not to annoy the birds.

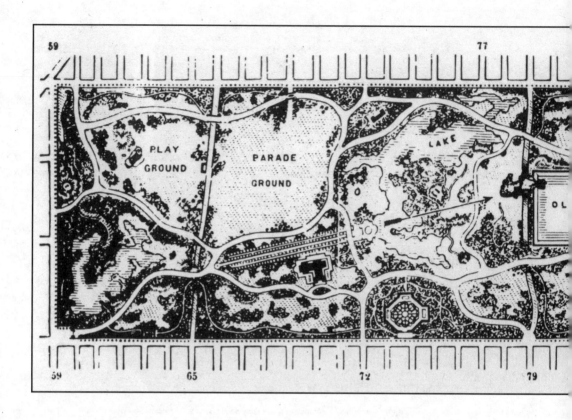

And he trained twenty-four men, called park keepers, to teach and enforce the rules. Each day, the gray-suited park keepers practiced patrolling the paths, awaiting visitors.

Though drained by his park duties, Fred kept his promise to look after John Hull's family. Mary had moved the children (John Charles, Charlotte, and Owen) to New York City, and Fred visited them often.

Friends for years, Fred and Mary decided to get married in 1859. The new family moved into an

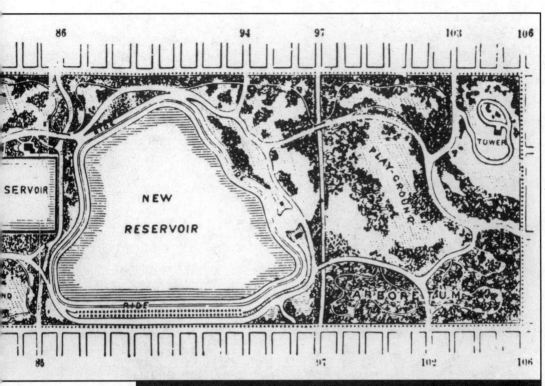

Fred and Calvert's original 1858 plan, Greensward, was chosen over thirty-two competitors as the best design for Central Park.

apartment near Fred's office, and Fred struggled to support a family of five.

Money troubles loomed at the park as well. Construction costs were higher than the planners expected. One commissioner, Andrew Green, became park accountant to watch expenses. Green, though honest and hardworking, distrusted everyone. To cut costs, he reduced wages and fired laborers–yet

Workers hauled millions of cartloads of rocks out of the park and hauled in thousands of pounds of rich soil, trees, and bushes.

ordered foremen to finish jobs faster. He decided that one office was using too many pencils and refused to buy more. Getting enough money to do his job became a daily struggle for Fred. He suffered from headaches and lack of sleep.

But Fred rejoiced in June 1860 when his first son, John Theodore, was born. Eight weeks later, he took Mary and the baby out for a drive. The worn-out man fell asleep at the reins and the horse bolted, tipping the buggy. The family was flung to the pavement. Mary and baby John were unhurt, but Fred's shattered thighbone pierced his pants. The doctor predicted that Fred, already weak from overwork, would die within a week. Then little John fell ill from infant cholera, perhaps from polluted city water. When John died, sorrow added to Fred's pain.

Somehow, Fred found strength to recover. While his leg mended, Mary drove him through the park to check on his crews. Andrew Green's power had grown during Fred's two-month absence. Green expected exact lists of every expense, yet he would not hire workers to keep the accounts. Fred had to check with Green before making any decisions; he could not even have the grass mowed or a bridge repaired without his approval. Green's penny-pinching, Fred feared, would damage the park.

By late winter of 1861, Fred could hobble around the park on crutches. One evening, he visited the skating pond, already a popular gathering spot. As he inched along the icy path, a smile spread below his handlebar moustache. Hundreds of New Yorkers, rich and poor, were enjoying the frozen lake. Skaters glided past snow-whitened trees planted by Fred's crews, and onlookers viewed a scene of natural beauty he and Calvert had only imagined a few years ago.

Ice skating became a popular winter sport as soon as Central Park's lake was finished. (This photo is from 1894.)

New Yorkers were becoming quite proud of their new park. It was changing their lives and how they looked at their city. And people in other cities were watching the Central Park experiment. Did their cities need parks? Would this new idea of public places to rest and play catch on? Fred hoped so.

There was work left to finish on Central Park, Fred knew. Piles of stone still littered the ground, and some fields had not yet been planted. But the bitter fights over money were sapping Fred's energy. He was worried, too, about the growing anger between northerners and southerners over slavery. What would happen if the nation broke into civil war?

Fred loved building Central Park. He told Calvert, "It occupied my whole heart." But perhaps the time was coming, he thought, to move on again.

4

Too Wonderful
to Be Believed

When the Civil War erupted in 1861, Fred was thirty-eight years old with a bad limp. The Union army would not take him, but a friend offered him a chance to serve. Reverend Henry Bellows was president of the US Sanitary Commission, a group led by doctors and scientists determined to help soldiers stay healthy. The huge Central Park construction job showed Bellows that his friend had a genius for organizing. Would he run the commission in Washington, DC?

Leaving Calvert to finish Central Park (and fight with Andrew Green), Fred moved his family to the Union capital. Immediately he inspected the troops around the city. The disordered camps shocked him. Soldiers, many just teens from small towns and farms, lacked training to fight. Worse, fresh food and clean water were hard to find. The dirty conditions meant the men risked cholera and other diseases that often swept through crowded cities. Fred knew that illness could be more deadly in war than bullets.

Fred often worked late into the night during the Civil War, studying reports and designing ways to keep soldiers clean and healthy.

Rushing to save lives, Fred sent out dozens of sanitary inspectors. Checklists in hand, they made sure hospitals and camps had enough food, water, medicine, blankets, and other essential supplies. The

Troops crowded into tent cities suffered from diseases and discomforts just like poor people living in unhealthy slums.

commission sought donations to fill in the gaps. The first battles revealed that more doctors, nurses, and bed space were also needed. So Fred organized a mininavy of ferries, tugboats, and fishing craft refitted to carry wounded men from battlefields to hospital ships he designed. President Lincoln praised the commission's efforts as "a work of great humanity, and of great practical value to the nation, in this time of trial."

Yet the war spread and casualties mounted. Fred pushed himself harder than ever. His face grew lined and his hair thinned. "He works like a dog all day and sits up nearly all night," a coworker wrote in his diary, "sleeps on a sofa in his clothes, and breakfasts on *strong coffee and pickles!!!*" No wonder Fred sometimes lost his temper and suffered stomachaches and dizzy spells. His small salary and old debts gave him another worry. Fred wrote Reverend Bellows, "If I should die, my wife and children would be in absolute poverty." Something had to change.

A possibility opened in 1863 with an offer to manage a mine complex in California. Two hundred miles east of San Francisco, the Mariposa had seven gold mines, four mills for crushing ore, a railroad, and almost seventy square miles of land. As Mariposa's manager, Fred would make $10,000 a year in gold—four times his commission salary. His health broken by the war, in debt with a wife and four children (including a new baby, Marion) to support, Fred took the job.

A cloud of red dust swirled around Fred's carriage on the long road to Mariposa. The parched, almost treeless plain he crossed looked dead compared to the lush eastern forests. He finally reached Mariposa headquarters in Bear Valley at nightfall. The one rocky street, lined with shabby stores, stables, and saloons, looked gloomy in the fading light.

For the next five weeks, Fred rode through Mariposa studying the estate. Some mines looked abandoned. Machines needed repairs, and timbers bracing the tunnels were crumbling. Chances for a rich strike did not look good.

But one day, Fred climbed down a mineshaft to inspect the veins of ore. Knocking off a chunk of quartz, he held a candle up to the rock. Flecks of gold glittered in the flickering light.

Fred wrote to Mary, urging her to bring the children. His letter also warned, "You must be prepared for a very hard life." Their only neighbors would be miners—men who wore guns to breakfast. In Fred's first three days, a store was robbed and two men were stabbed. But the weather was the worst news. September temperatures soared to 110°F, and the wind "seems to come out of an oven."

While waiting for his family to make the long journey, Fred worked to improve the estate. He ordered construction of a new mill and much-needed repairs. Geologists were sent searching for new veins of gold. To crush more rock, the mills needed more waterpower, so Fred drew plans to build a canal. To improve the lives of miners, he lowered prices at the company stores, planned a reading room, and invited a doctor to move to Mariposa.

Most of the changes cost money, and the mines were not yet producing enough gold to pay for them. So he cut the miners' wages to lower costs—from $3.50 to $3.15 a day. The miners rebelled by striking for five days. Olmsted refused to budge, and most of the men picked up their tools again. Troubled but still optimistic, Fred pinned his hopes on a new mine that experts said would be rich.

The family arrived with the spring rains. Home was a roomy apartment over a company store. Bear Valley had no school, so the children were free to roam the Sierra Nevada foothills. Fred often joined them on his bay, Dash. Riding over hills of wildflowers with the children on their burros (Kitty, Fanny, and Beppo), care lines eased on his face and Fred grew fonder of the California landscape.

Summer heat drove the family out of Mariposa to visit Yosemite Valley, a two-day ride east into the cool mountains. The Olmsteds had read early explorers' descriptions of Yosemite's natural wonders. Leaving dust-choked Bear Valley behind, the travelers were refreshed by the tangy scent of mountain

Stereoview photographs by Carleton Watkins gave most people their first 3-D look at the spectacular beauty of California's Yosemite Valley.

pine forests. Though anxious to reach Yosemite, they could not resist camping near the giant sequoias in the Mariposa Big Tree Grove. The 250-foot-tall sequoias looked to Fred like "strangers from another world." He and eleven-year-old John Charles tried to stretch their arms around the ancient cinnamon-colored trunks. Fred told Mary that these were the grandest trees he had ever seen.

On August 13, 1864, the trail brought the family to Inspiration Point. Nothing Fred had seen before prepared him for the beauty of Yosemite Valley. Granite cliffs nearly a mile high loomed over a broad green

Marion, Charlotte, John Charles, and Owen did not attend school in Mariposa and had plenty of time to play outdoors and ride their burros.

river valley dotted with trees. Waterfalls, higher and more delicate than Niagara, cascaded down the steep walls. Even the jagged, overhanging cliffs looked peaceful behind a soft, misty haze. In his notebook, Fred called Yosemite "too wonderful to be believed."

The family spent blissful weeks exploring Yosemite, picnicking and collecting fossils. Fred and John Charles climbed to the top of a 12,764-foot peak. But Fred returned to bad news in Mariposa. The new mine yielded far less gold than expected. The Civil War dragged on too. His optimism faded.

One shining bit of luck was not gold but a new law. In the midst of the bloody war, President Lincoln had signed a historic bill, giving the Yosemite Valley and the Mariposa Big Tree Grove to California—for a wilderness park! Frederick Law Olmsted, respected designer of Central Park, was chosen to head the new Yosemite Commission, to plan a park "for public use, resort and recreation...inalienable for all time."

Fred inspected the struggling mines by day and worked long after dark on plans for Yosemite. He could imagine a time when millions of people would visit the valley from all over the country and the world. Cramming the park with roads, shops, hotels, and restaurants for the tourists would destroy scenery Fred called "the greatest glory of nature." Unlike the

Central Park site, he believed, the Yosemite landscape should not be changed. The natural valley would inspire visitors more than anything a park designer could create. Somehow, the park must preserve the grandeur while still allowing people to experience it.

As Fred shaped his Yosemite ideas into a report, a bank threatened to take the Mariposa mines to repay company debts. The only solution was to lease

This stereoview shows visitors to the Mariposa Big Tree Grove posed by a tree to show the astonishing size of giant sequoias.

the estate to another company, leaving Fred without a job. He took gold bars from the company safe to pay his back salary, then returned to the Yosemite report.

The valley must be open to all, he argued, not just the wealthy. A stagecoach road should be built to reach it, with spots to rest and admire the views. But to protect the quiet valley floor, only one narrow carriage lane should loop around the edge. And instead of fancy hotels, there should be cabins and campsites with only "simple necessities." Only by preserving the valley's natural glories, he believed, would it continue to refresh bodies and minds. He wrote, it is the duty of government to protect Yosemite for people today–and forever. Politicians and other leaders gathered in Yosemite on August 9, 1865, to hear Olmsted read the report. But he was not certain–did they listen?

Unsettled and unemployed, Fred was cheered by letters from his old partner, Calvert Vaux. Since Fred had left New York, Calvert had struggled to complete Central Park, including sixty-five acres added in 1863. Fights with Andrew Green had finally forced Calvert to leave the park, but he wanted to return. Fred should come back, too, Calvert wrote. Together they could protect their creation. With New York's booming economy, at least they wouldn't have to fight to get money.

US Speaker of the House Schuyler Colfax camped in Yosemite with Fred, Mary, and others interested in protecting the valley and opening it to visitors.

Letter after letter urged Fred to rejoin their partnership. The triumph of Central Park had won the men national–even international–fame. With the Civil War over, Calvert thought growing cities would want to build parks as well as offices and factories. Calvert reminded Fred that he was an artist, not a miner. Designing beautiful landscapes was what God meant for him to do. If Fred returned to New York, Calvert wrote, "We may have some fun together yet."

If he left California, Fred worried, what would happen to Yosemite? But then he thought about Central Park. "I love it all through," he wrote Calvert. "There is no other place in the world that is as much home to me." He had made enough money to repay the debts to his father. He could afford to return to the work he loved.

5

Park Keeping

On clear fall Sundays in 1865, visitors streamed into Central Park. High-tailed horses pulled in carriages driven by men wearing top hats. Ladies trotted in riding sidesaddle. Couples on foot pushed baby carriages or strolled arm in arm. And children wearing moth-eaten mufflers raced inside to jump in piles of golden leaves.

Forty-three-year-old Fred may have felt like running and leaping too. Calvert had convinced the park commissioners to rehire the partners as Central Park's landscape architects. Fred had a fresh chance to make sure the park lived up to his dreams.

Crowds of playing children have fun but can trample park grass.

As weeks passed, though, he recognized growing problems. Almost everyone seemed to want space for a favorite activity. Baseball players wanted ball fields, carriage drivers wanted racetracks, and art lovers wanted museums. The partners opposed the changes, believing that every chunk of land taken over would be a loss to the whole.

Some pushed especially hard for a zoo. A temporary menagerie in the park already housed deer, bald eagles, cockatoos, monkeys, and Cape buffalo. Pressured by the commission, Fred and Calvert finally agreed to design a zoo. But they insisted it be constructed on land outside the park. To them, keeping the park beautiful was as important as building it.

But protecting Central Park was not their only job. Just as Calvert had predicted, cities all over the country now wanted parks like New York City's. Some wanted parks as showplaces of their town's wealth. But others saw that parks relieved crowding and improved health, as Fred believed. Brooklyn, Albany, Philadelphia, Chicago, and San Francisco asked for advice or park plans. Other clients requested landscape plans for college campuses, cemeteries, and hospital grounds.

One of the partners visited each new job site, getting to know the land and how it would be used.

After developing a general plan, the partners hired engineers, architects, gardeners, and draftsmen to help work out details and draw final plans. The office of Olmsted, Vaux & Company, at 110 Broadway, had more than enough projects to keep both work-addicted partners busy.

The Olmsted family lived on Staten Island, a short ferry ride from the Brooklyn park project. California had drawn the family together, and Fred made time for rowing and other outings with the children. In June 1866, Fred's father arrived for a visit. One day he toured the Brooklyn site with Fred.

Construction had not yet begun on Prospect Park, but Fred could describe the rolling meadows, tumbling creeks, and rustic footbridges the firm had drawn for the plan. Blessed with broader spaces than in Central Park, and inspired by wild California landscapes, the designers pursued a bolder vision. The chief goal of the space, wrote Fred, was "a sense of enlarged freedom," a place for people of all classes "to come together for the single purpose of enjoyment." And bringing everyone together in one peaceful setting would be good for the whole city—good for democracy itself. Elderly John Olmsted must have felt deep pride in how his son used nature to build a human community.

But soon after his father's visit, Fred got word from California. Yosemite's commissioners refused to spend state money to protect the valley. Fred's ideas for stopping damage by tourists were being ignored. Hotels, roads, cattle, and fences already scarred the valley. Fred was furious—but too far away to do anything about it.

He also had more troubles in New York. As still more people used the park, some complained about strict rules. A newspaper cartoon showed disappointed children surrounded by signs: "Don't Pick the Flowers" and "Keep Off the Grass." A loving father, Fred appreciated playgrounds and children's games more than most. But a park could be used to death. Fred realized that New York needed parks all over the city, with lots of room for many different activities. And, he believed, the parks should be connected by broad, tree-lined roads. The roads, which Fred called parkways, could bring natural scenery and sweet, clean air deep into the city. Instead of being separate islands surrounded by buildings, the parks should tie the city together.

But there was not much land left in New York City. And most city leaders thought parks were decorations—pretty, but not important like offices, schools, and factories. Fred and Calvert wrote reports and

This 1869 newspaper cartoon shows that some people thought rules to protect Central Park's plants and quiet setting spoiled visitors' fun.

drew plans to change their minds. A few parks and parkways were built, but most of New York's last acres were soon built over.

Still determined, Fred looked for another place to test the partners' ideas. In August 1868, he visited Buffalo, New York, to choose a site for a grand city park. From the carriage, Fred could see that Buffalo still had some open land. But hammering in

Families flocked to Prospect Park to boat on Brooklyn's only lake and to relax in a green oasis inside the growing city.

the distance meant more buildings were on the way. Many assumed that Buffalo, like other cities, was doomed to ugliness.

But Fred saw a solution. City growth, he said, should be planned around open spaces. Instead of picking one park site, Fred proposed three parks, and his plan connected them by parkways. Then Buffalo would not feel cramped like other big cities. And Buffalo's citizens, even the poorest, would never feel too far from nature. The city planners were convinced. When Fred returned home, he and Calvert set to work designing for Buffalo the nation's first system of city parks.

It was a great success from the start. No one had believed a city could be so pleasant.

For their first city park system, Fred and Calvert designed the lake, woods, and meadows of Delaware Park to be Buffalo's Central Park.

On one of many trips to Buffalo in 1869, Fred decided to visit nearby Niagara Falls. As a child, the magnificent sight had filled him with awe. Now Fred felt sick. The Niagara River's once-wild shores were fouled with trinket shops, cheap hotels, and advertising signs. Landowners charged fees for a peek at the falls. Tourism, which Fred feared would damage Yosemite, was destroying Niagara Falls. He was too far away to protect Yosemite, but Fred vowed to fight for Niagara Falls.

Yet once again Central Park demanded his attention. In 1869, a group of politicians known as Tammany Hall took control of the New York City government. Tammany Hall thought the park should show off the city's wealth and achievements—not give people a healthy place to enjoy nature.

The park again became a huge construction site. Thousands of workers were hired in exchange for their votes. They stripped branches off trees, smoothed rough ground, and replaced native plants with flower beds. Plans were drawn for a conservatory, an opera house, a fancy zoo (Fred and Calvert's plan was forgotten), and other grand buildings.

Tammany's new, poorly trained park keepers failed to enforce park rules. Vandals stole plants and broke equipment. Visitors had to dodge speeding carriages and put up with noise, litter, and crime.

Fred and Calvert were horrified. But the new commissioners would not meet with them to hear their complaints. In November 1870, both were fired.

Fred's only happiness that year came from his family. At forty-eight, he was overjoyed to have a new son. Young Henry might someday follow in his father's footsteps as a landscape architect. A few years later, Fred even changed the boy's name to Frederick Law Olmsted Jr.

In 1871, *The New York Times* published evidence that Tammany Hall politicians were stealing millions of city dollars. The scandal rocked New York, tossing Tammany out of power. Andrew Green was appointed city accountant to clear up the money mess, and Fred and Calvert were rehired to repair Central Park.

Once again, the partners worked side by side on their park. But there was tension between them. Articles in newspapers and magazines often gave Fred most of the credit for the park's design. Calvert was jealous and blamed Fred, while Fred resented Calvert's anger. He thought he had always treated Calvert fairly. In October 1871, Fred and Calvert ended their partnership. Although both stayed on as Central Park's designers, Fred took on more of the responsibilities for maintaining the park.

Three months later, Fred was at work when a telegram arrived, urging him to rush to Hartford. He reached home in time to say good-bye to his dying father. Fred wrote to a friend, "A kinder father never lived."

Fred could not stop working to mourn. Tammany Hall was regaining strength. He raced to replant and to retrain the park keepers, but each year the city gave him less money. By 1877, Tammany politicians controlled the park board. To get rid of Fred, the board proclaimed that the park was complete. On January 5, 1878, more than twenty years after his arrival, Fred was kicked out of Central Park.

Dozens of Fred's friends protested the firing in New York's newspapers. Though Calvert was not dismissed, many doubted that he could protect the park alone. Fred, his health broken from work and conflict, followed doctor's orders to take a long vacation.

6

Painting with Lakes and Trees

Niagara Falls thundered again in Fred's ears. Goat Island, where he walked, was a forested rock between the American and Canadian sides of the Niagara River. Linked to the New York side by only a footbridge, the wooded island had escaped the frenzy of building that claimed the riverbanks.

For years, a few Americans and Canadians had voiced outrage at the eyesores built around Niagara Falls. European tourists criticized North Americans for destroying one of their greatest treasures.

Electricity generated by Niagara Falls powered mills that poured pollution into the river.

At last in 1878, Canada's governor-general invited New York State to help create an international park. This was a startling new idea: a park shared by two nations. New York governor Lucius Robinson asked Fred and James Gardner to report on the condition of the falls. From Goat Island, Fred realized how much damage had been done.

The report described a view of "solid ugliness." The river was lined with "mills, carpenter shops, stables, 'bazaars,' ice-houses, laundries with clothes hanging out to dry, bath houses [and] large, glaring white hotels." To others, it must have looked hopeless. How could a park preserve scenery that was already destroyed?

But Fred could see what others could not. The solution was to restore the land—an exciting new approach. The state should purchase a mile-long strip along the New York shore above the falls, plus the still-wild islands in the river. Buildings should be demolished and the grounds replanted with native wildflowers, bushes, and trees. Nothing artificial—stores, statues, flower beds—should be allowed.

Just like Fred's Yosemite report, the Niagara paper argued that the people of today have a duty to future generations. Natural treasures should be saved for all people, always, not just a few of today's "money-getters."

Not everyone in New York agreed. Shop and hotel owners along the river objected loudly to losing their businesses. The state's new governor insisted that seeing Niagara Falls was a luxury. Why should taxpayers pay for a park?

Niagara's defenders needed public support. Fred and influential friends began a publicity campaign, urging everyone they knew to write letters and newspaper articles about saving Niagara. Restoring the falls would be a long battle, but Fred vowed to stick with it.

Of course, it was not his only project. He was in demand as the nation's leading landscape architect. Besides building Mount Royal Park in Montreal, Canada, he was landscaping the grounds of the US Capitol and beginning plans for several important parks in Boston. Final drawings were carefully inked in the neat first-floor office of his family's New York City brownstone. Next to Fred sat his stepson, John Charles, eagerly practicing the drafting skills he needed to join the family business.

In 1883, chances for restoring Niagara improved. A new governor, Grover Cleveland, backed the idea. Still, the state legislators had to be convinced.

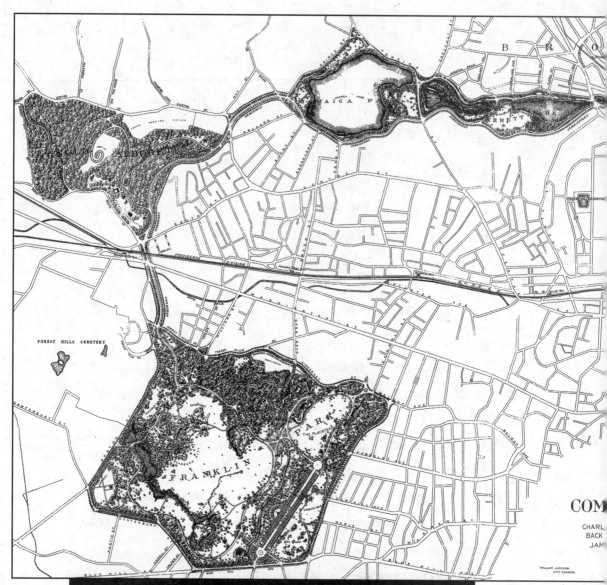

Fred's plan for Boston's park system stretched around the city,
so all residents could easily escape to open space and fresh air.

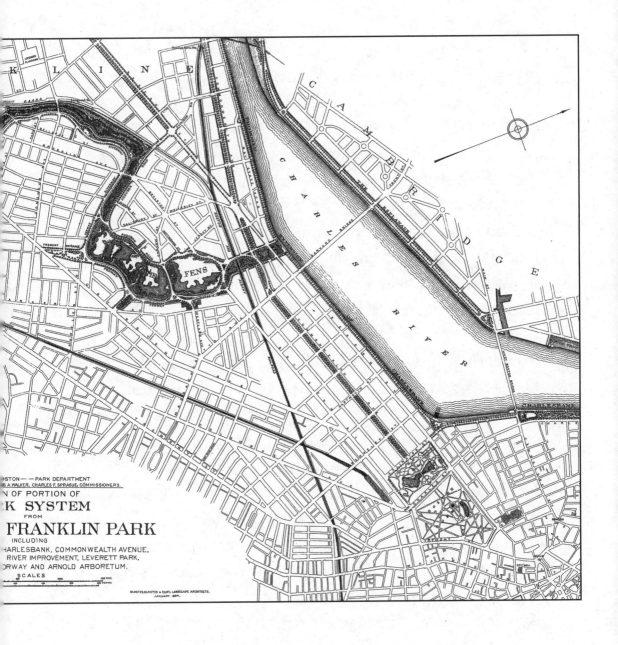

N OF PORTION OF

K SYSTEM

FROM

FRANKLIN PARK

INCLUDING

HARLESBANK, COMMONWEALTH AVENUE,
RIVER IMPROVEMENT, LEVERETT PARK,
ORWAY AND ARNOLD ARBORETUM.

SCALES

OLMSTED,OLMSTED & ELIOT, LANDSCAPE ARCHITECTS,
JANUARY 1894.

It would take all the public pressure Fred and other park supporters could rally. They formed a new group called the Niagara Falls Association, which blanketed the state with articles, petitions, and pamphlets. New Yorkers responded by wiring and writing the legislature, demanding that a park be created.

On April 30, 1883, the legislators authorized the land purchase in a bill signed by Governor Cleveland. But who would design the park? Fred's old foe Andrew Green belonged to the Niagara Falls Commission. Green vetoed Fred as designer.

The rejection smarted and gave Fred another reason to get away from New York. That spring, the Olmsteds bought a new home close to Fred's Boston work. The rambling farmhouse was in Brookline–a countrylike suburb just a short trolley ride from the city. Naming the place Fairsted, Fred enlarged the house and turned the yard into a miniature park. It was the first time he owned ground to plant since selling the farm. With their money woes over and doctor's orders for Fred to work less, the Olmsteds enjoyed parties with their neighbors and a new treat—two grandsons (stepdaughter Charlotte's sons).

Yet work kept piling up, including designs for the campus at Stanford University and George Vanderbilt's splendid Biltmore estate. Vanderbilt's

Fred's vision turned the grounds of Biltmore Mansion into formal gardens, working farms, a forestry school, and 80,000 acres of mountain forest.

wealth gave Fred the chance to create all he imagined, unlimited by tight city budgets. Though his joints now ached with age, Fred rode horseback through the Biltmore forest to make sure crews completed every detail to perfection.

To keep up with everything, Fred hired other designers and draftsmen. He also proudly took on a new partner–John Charles. Rooms were added to Fairsted to make office space for everyone.

With all the work, Fred needed well-trained assistants. No schools yet taught landscape architecture, so Fred designed a training program for young men. Students were required to take tough university courses in architecture, horticulture, engineering, and drawing. He assigned stacks of books to read and plans to copy.

A bearded Olmsted stands beside Biltmore owner George Vanderbilt and the crew who dug, shaped, and planted the vast estate.

But the students' favorite part of training was trailing Mr. Olmsted around a park site. Watching their teacher study the plants, soil, and shape of the land, they learned how he worked with nature to make each park unique. Fred advised each one to keep learning on his own, as he had. Become "professor to yourself."

One young apprentice was especially dear to Fred: his son, Frederick Jr. Rick often accompanied his father to Biltmore's forests. "What is better worth doing well," asked Fred, "than the planting of trees?"

Then in 1886, the Niagara Falls Commission overturned Andrew Green. Fred and his former part-ner, Calvert Vaux, were asked to design the Niagara State Reservation. The aging artists worked together

In Franklin Park, Fred set aside some spaces for visitors to enjoy sports and games, and other spaces to find countrylike quiet.

once again, this time restoring the natural area around the falls. Their design was applauded worldwide. When Canada dedicated its Niagara park, in 1888, the dream of an international nature preserve became a reality. Thousands had contributed to this triumph. But without Fred, said one campaigner, "there would be no State Reservation at Niagara today."

At the same time, the Boston parks were taking shape. Fred told his partners, "Nothing else compares in importance to us with the Boston work." Their first project began as a stinking mudflat, polluted with sewage from the city. Engineering and artistry

The once-foul Back Bay Fens became a place where people could relax from daily stresses and feel their spirits lift.

transformed it into the Back Bay Fens, a salt marsh crossed by a crooked stream for boating. Jamaica Pond was already a lovely natural lake; Olmsted gracefully framed it with trees and pathways. When Harvard University wanted a living museum of trees, Fred grouped the plants so visitors could study their beauty as well as their scientific value. Together, the Boston parks and connecting parkways stretched seven green miles through the city and won the name the Emerald Necklace.

The system's crown jewel was Franklin Park. In the bustling 1880s, Fred knew that city dwellers needed places for active recreation. About one-third of the design featured space for athletic fields, tennis and ball games, a music amphitheater, and a Little Folks Fair for small children. But two-thirds of Franklin Park was reserved for country scenery, with thick forests, broad meadows, and open skies like the Connecticut Fred roamed as a boy.

After a lifetime of hard work, illness, and grief, Fred felt more deeply than ever that people need the physical and spiritual relief that nature brings. His blue eyes could still see far into the future, to a world of fast-growing cities with towering buildings, deafening traffic, and rushing crowds. Every year, people would need parks more and more.

It took engineering and heavy machinery in the 1890s to sculpt the Muddy River into a connecting parkway for the Emerald Necklace.

By 1920, nature had healed the construction scars, working
with Fred to create the Riverway Park for canoeing, strolling,
and horseback riding.

Many called the Emerald Necklace Fred's masterpiece, but he never stopped fighting to protect his first park. In 1892, Tammany Hall politicians and some wealthy horse owners pushed for the construction of a seventy-foot-wide racetrack in Central Park. Calling the track "unjust and immoral," Fred helped raise a public outcry. The track was canceled. For Fred, the victory was sweet.

Fred and architect Daniel Burnham designed Chicago's 1893 Columbian Exposition to show millions of people how splendid a city can be.

Also sweet were the honors and praise showered on the balding, gray-bearded man for his dedication and achievements. In 1893, seventy-one-year-old Fred was delighted by two scholarly awards. The boy who never attended college had grown up to receive honorary doctor of letters degrees from Harvard and Yale on the same day. Each award recognized Fred for leading the nation in bringing the beauties of nature into city life and preserving the country's natural treasures.

Fred valued the tributes of friends and fellow artists most. Famed architect Daniel Burnham called him an artist who "paints with lakes and wooded slopes; with lawns and banks and forest-covered hills; with mountainsides and ocean views." But perhaps his most cherished honor was a friend's book on trees, dedicated to "Frederick Law Olmsted, the great artist whose love for Nature has been a priceless benefit to his fellow-countrymen."

To honor the artist who painted with lakes and trees, John
Singer Sargent painted Fred in the Biltmore gardens he designed.

Afterword

After almost forty years as a park maker, Fred was forced to retire by illnesses and memory loss. His last five years passed at McLean Hospital, in Massachusetts, on peaceful grounds he designed years before. Fred died on August 28, 1903, with Frederick Law Olmsted Jr. at his side.

Fred's son and stepson carried his name and vision into the twentieth century. From their office at Fairsted, the Olmsted brothers created parks, suburban communities, grounds for hospitals, universities, and state capitols, and park systems for cities throughout the nation. Frederick Jr. expanded his father's vision for Yosemite, helping to create the National Park Service. In writings that would have filled his father with pride, the younger Olmsted argued the nation's parks should save wildlife, forests, and natural beauty "unimpaired for the enjoyment of future generations."

Over the decades, many Olmsted parks have been overused, neglected, built over bit by bit, even destroyed. But determined individuals and groups are working to protect and restore them. The Central Park Conservancy, founded in 1980, is dedicated to

As Fred foresaw, cities grew up around his urban parks. Every year people need Central Park and other green spaces more and more.

restoring the Greensward Plan and keeping it alive. In Boston, the Emerald Necklace Conservancy invites families to help with tree plantings and cleanups in their favorite green spaces. At Fairsted, the National Park Service invites children into the Olmsteds' workshop to learn how to draft plans for parks of their own imagining. Protecting and extending Olmsted's legacy is a growing national movement.

An environmentalist before the word was coined, Frederick Law Olmsted believed that nature's beauty heals the body and lifts the human spirit, strengthening our communities and our civilization. His parks are living monuments to his ideas.

In 1892, Fred's love of travel took him to France for new landscape design ideas and to England for a happy family reunion.

US Conservation Time Line

1822–Frederick Law Olmsted born, Hartford, Connecticut
1826–Publication of *The Birds of America* by John James Audubon
1850–Olmsted visits Birkenhead Park, Liverpool, England
1858–Olmsted and Vaux's Greensward Plan wins the design
contest for Central Park

New Yorkers love Central Park.

1865–Olmsted writes report to the Yosemite Commission on
preserving Yosemite and the Mariposa Big Trees
1868–Olmsted and Vaux begin planning the Buffalo park system
1872–First National Park established–Yellowstone
1878–Olmsted begins designing Boston's connected parks,
later called the Emerald Necklace
1886–Niagara Falls Reservation, designed by Olmsted and
Vaux, opens to the public
1892–Sierra Club founded by John Muir
1902–Publication of *How to Build Up Worn Out Soils* by George
Washington Carver

Niagara Falls thrills visitors.

1903–Olmsted dies, Belmont, Massachusetts

1903–Beginning of National Wildlife Refuge System–Pelican Island, Florida

1905–US Forest Service established

1910–Camp Fire Girls and Boy Scouts of America founded

1914–Last known passenger pigeon dies in zoo; four years later, last known Carolina parakeet dies at same place

1924–First US National Wilderness Area set aside–the Gila Wilderness

1933–Civilian Conservation Corps (CCC) created to give young men jobs and conserve natural resources

1949–Publication of *A Sand County Almanac* by Aldo Leopold

1962–Publication of *Silent Spring* by Rachel Carson

1964–Wilderness Act

1970–First Earth Day; Clean Air Act; Creation of US Environmental Protection Agency (EPA)

1972–Marine Protection Act

1973–Endangered Species Act

1977–Clean Water Act

2006–The film *An Inconvenient Truth* released on global climate change

2008–Intergovernmental Panel on Climate Change (IPCC) finds global warming trends largely caused by and can be reduced by human activities

Glossary

abolitionist: a person who works to abolish slavery

arboretum: a place where trees and other plants are grown for scientific and educational purposes

architect: a person who designs structures such as buildings and bridges

giant sequoia: an evergreen tree that can live 3,500 years and grow over 250 feet tall

landscape architect: a person who designs outdoor spaces, such as parks and school grounds

national park: a place set aside by a national government to protect its natural beauty, history, or scientific value

parkway: a broad, tree-lined road through a city

rural area: the country or farm country; not part of the city

suburban area: a smaller community outside a city, between city and country

urban area: a city or large community; not part of the country

Places to Visit

Great Lakes and Canada
- Belle Isle Park–Detroit, Michigan
- Jackson Park–Chicago, Illinois
- Mount Royal Park–Montreal, Quebec

Massachusetts
- Arnold Arboretum–Boston, Massachusetts
- Franklin Park–Boston, Massachusetts
- Frederick Law Olmsted National Historic Site–Brookline, Massachusetts

New York
- Central Park–New York, New York
- Delaware Park–Buffalo, New York
- Niagara Falls State Park–Niagara, New York
- Prospect Park–Brooklyn, New York

South
- Biltmore Estate–Asheville, North Carolina
- Cherokee Park–Louisville, Kentucky
- US Capitol grounds–Washington, DC

West
- Mountain View Cemetery–Oakland, California
- Stanford University–Stanford, California
- Yosemite National Park–Yosemite, California

Take It Outside

Make art for parks. How do landscape architects imagine what a park will look like? Often, they start by sketching. Take paper outside and draw what you see. You can sharpen your focus by making a frame with your fingers or some cardboard. Hold the frame in various positions and draw what you see inside the boundaries. What do you like about the scene—trees, rocks, creeks, buildings? What would you like to change? Now sketch the scene a few times, trying out different possibilities. Use color to see how leaves and flowers and snow could change the scene through the seasons. Which park would you like best?

Map your funshed. A watershed is the area of land where rain washes into a particular river or bay. A funshed is the area where you can go to have fun outside. Start by finding outdoor play areas close to where you live: your backyard, apartment courtyard, or townhouse common space. Then start making a map of places nearby you can walk to—pocket parks, school grounds, community greens. Can you add more local parks, pick-your-own-produce farms, or fishing spots that you could reach by bike? With an adult's help, your map could include state and regional parks, wildlife refuges, nature sanctuaries, and even national parks you can reach by car or public transportation. The more green play spaces you map, the more fun you can have in your funshed.

Design a Greensward for your school. Wouldn't it be great if a park surrounded every school? Get a group together to walk your school grounds—what natural features are already there that you want to keep: a stream? Some woods? Some rolling hills? What could be added to increase the beauty and fun of the space: a small pond for frog-watching? Boulders for climbing? Wildflowers for studying butterflies? Everyone can brainstorm ideas, then get out a huge piece of paper and design together like Fred and Calvert. Or start a competition: who can come up with the best plan for making school grounds more beautiful, healthful, and fun?

Be a park maker. No matter how small, almost any space can be made greener and more parklike. You can add a potted plant and a seat to your balcony, or set up a birdbath and plant bushes to bring birds to your yard. Ask at your school if you can help plant trees to make the playground shadier, or if an unused patch of asphalt can be pulled up and replanted with meadow grasses. Is there a vacant lot that's turning into a trash heap? Get permission to clean it up with a Scout troop or some friends, then collect logs, rocks, flower seeds, saplings, and other natural objects to make the space your own. Remember to make curving pathways through the space so that visitors can enjoy every part of your park.

Be a park keeper. How sad to see a beautiful park neglected and abused. Well, fix it up! Tote along a recycling bag when you hike a path or watch a soccer game and collect old bottles and cans. Remind your friends not to toss snack wrappers on the ground or leave fishing line caught on a branch. Check your park's headquarters about events such as weed pulling, trail clearing, or bench painting. Does your park need money for more trees or special programs? Organize a fund-raising event such as a yard sale. And if people in your neighborhood forget the importance of your park, remind them. Write letters to your newspaper and to local politicians. Tell others why parks are important—today and tomorrow.

To Learn More

Central Park Conservancy, www.centralparknyc.org

Emerald Necklace Conservancy, www.emeraldnecklace.org

Frederick Law Olmsted National Historic Site, www.nps.gov/
   frla/index.htm

National Association of Olmsted Parks, www.olmsted.org

Olmsted and America's Urban Parks, www.theolmstedlegacy.com

Yosemite Conservancy, www.yosemiteconservancy.org

Fred's home and landscape architecture office in
Brookline, Massachusetts, is now the Frederick Law
Olmsted National Historic Site.

Major Sources

Allen, David Grayson. *The Olmsted National Historic Site and the Growth of Historic Landscape Preservation.* Boston: Northeastern Univ. Press, 2007.

Olmsted, Frederick Law. *A Journey in the Seaboard Slave States.* New York: Dix & Edward, 1856.

Olmsted, Frederick Law. *Walks and Talks of an American Farmer in England.* New York: Putnam and Company, 1852.

Olmsted, Frederick Law Jr., and Theodora Kimball, eds. *Forty Years of Landscape Architecture.* New York: Putnam's Sons, 1928.

Roper, Laura Wood. *FLO: A Biography of Frederick Law Olmsted.* Baltimore, MD: Johns Hopkins University, 1973.

Rosenzweig, Roy, and Elizabeth Blackmar. *The Park and the People: A History of Central Park.* Ithaca, NY: Cornell Univ. Press, 1992.

Runte, Alfred. "Beyond the Spectacular: The Niagara Falls Preservation Campaign." *New York Historical Society Quarterly* 57 (1973): 30-50.

Rybczynski, Witold. *A Clearing in the Distance: Frederick Law Olmsted and America in the 19th Century.* New York: Scribner, 1999.

Zaitzevsky, Cynthia. *Frederick Law Olmsted and the Boston Park System.* Cambridge, MA: Belknap Press, 1982.

Index